NEIL ARMSTRONG

The Success of Apollo 11
and the First Man on the Moon

Written by Romain Parmentier
In collaboration with Romain Prévalet
Translated by Carly Probert

History 50MINUTES.com

NEIL ARMSTRONG

KEY INFORMATION

- **Born:** 5 August 1930 in Wapakoneta (Ohio)
- **Died:** 25 August 2012 in Cincinnati (Ohio)
- **Context:** Space race
- **Purpose of the mission:** To send men to the Moon
- **Areas of the universe explored:** Space and the Moon
- **Accomplishment:** He was the first man to set foot on the Moon and bring back sample material

INTRODUCTION

Throughout history, humans have contemplated the skies and the Moon in particular, which has always fascinated men to the point where they dreamed of one day setting foot on its surface. The space race of the 20th century finally presented an opportunity to do so. On 16 July 1969, from the US base at Cape Canaveral, the Saturn V rocket containing the Apollo 11 spaceship took off, carrying three astronauts, including Neil Armstrong. Destination: the Moon!

The United States prepared for such a feat for almost a decade. Entering into a race against the USSR during the Cold War (1945-1990), they fell behind in the space race and missed out on achieving a lot of firsts in the field. Nevertheless, the Americans were not deterred, having promised to be the first to arrive on the Moon, and to do so before the end of the 1960s. The honor of the nation was at stake.

The voyage of Apollo 11 to the Moon was unhindered. After four days, the spacecraft began orbiting the satellite. The final phase could begin. Returning to the lunar module with one of his companions, Neil Armstrong began the descent to the ground. Despite some technical problems, the crew landed on the Moon on 20 July 1969 at 8:17pm UTC. After more than six hours, Neil Armstrong ventured out of the spacecraft on 21 July and set foot on the ground, becoming the first man to walk on the moon. This was a major turning point in the history of mankind.

BIOGRAPHY

A LOVE FOR AVIATION AND AEROSPACE

Neil Armstrong was born on 5 August 1930 in Wapakoneta, Ohio. Born into a modest family, he quickly developed a passion for aviation and obtained his flying license on the day of his 16th birthday, before he even held a normal driving license. His family did not have the means to pay for his university studies, so Armstrong accepted a scholarship from the US Navy in exchange for service time in the army. Therefore, he enrolled at Purdue University (Indiana) in 1947, where he studied aeronautical engineering. But from 26 January 1949, he was forced to interrupt his studies to perform military service in the Navy. For 18 months, he attended pilot training on an aircraft carrier. He obtained his diploma in August 1950, shortly after the outbreak of the Korean War (1950-1953). In August 1951, still in service, Armstrong was set to the front, where he successfully completed 78 air missions. The following year, he was finally allowed to continue his studies, which he completed in 1955.

Photo of Neil Armstrong taken after a flight exercise in 1960.

The young man then began a career as a test pilot on jet aircrafts. He remained in this position until 1962, which allowed him to test high-performance engines, but also proved extremely dangerous. Meanwhile, the race for the conquest of space was heating up. After the exploits of the first American astronauts, Neil Armstrong decided to apply to NASA in 1962. Chosen to be a part of the NASA Astronaut Group 2, also called "New Nine", he was the first American civilian to become an astronaut. Subsequently, he participated in the *Gemini* program, aimed at mastering space flights, spacewalks and orbital maneuvers. On 20 September 1965, Neil Armstrong became the commander of *Gemini 8*, a prelude to the mission that made him famous.

Neil Armstrong wearing his exercise clothes for Gemini 2.

COMMANDER OF APOLLO 11

Alongside *Gemini*, NASA launched the Apollo program in 1961 with the aim of putting a man on the Moon. For eight years the missions followed one after another, moving the Americans closer to their goal. In 1969, everything seemed finally ready to reach the moon. Thanks to the rotation system of the Apollo crews, Neil Armstrong was given the command of the Apollo 11 mission to send man to the Moon. Furthermore, NASA also asked him to be the first to walk on the lunar surface.

For months, Neil Armstrong and his crew underwent extensive training to carry out their mission. Finally, on 16 July 1969, the astronaut took off onboard the rocket Saturn V. After separating from the successive modules of the spacecraft, Apollo 11 began its journey. After four days of transit, the crew reached the Moon. On 20 July 1969, the module landed without difficulty. At 2:56am on 21 July, Armstrong exited the spacecraft and became the first man to set foot on the Moon. After his triumphant success, the astronauts returned to Earth, where they became national heroes.

AFTER THE MOON LANDING

After the success of the Apollo 11 mission, Neil Armstrong decided not to return to space. He opted for a teaching career in the aerospace department of the University of Cincinnati until 1979. He was also part of several commissions of inquiry for NASA, namely inquiries about the incidents of the Apollo 13 mission in 1970 and the Space Shuttle Challenger in 1986.

Neil Armstrong died on 25 August 2012 at the age of 82 as a result of complications from cardiovascular surgery He will forever remain one of the greatest heroes in history.

POLITICAL, SOCIAL AND ECONOMIC CONTEXT

A WORLD PLUNGED INTO THE COLD WAR

In 1945, after the Second World War, the world was once again divided between two superpowers: the United States and the USSR. These two countries and their respective allies formed two separate blocs advocating opposing ideological and economic models: the Westerns promoted liberalism and the market economy, while the Soviets defended Communism and the planned economy. This international context, which marked the second half of the 20th century, did not however lead to a direct conflict between the US and the USSR, but a strong rivalry developed as one struggled to assert the superiority of one over the other.

This period, known as the Cold War, was characterized by a permanent state of tension and deterrence between the two blocs, without triggering an armed conflict of global proportions – which, at the time of the atomic bomb, would have been catastrophic. The two blocs nevertheless intervened militarily in peripheral conflicts, such as the Korean War, the Berlin crises (1949 and 1961) and the Vietnam War (1959-1975), inevitably exacerbating the climate of tension between them. In the sixties, the Cold War reached its peak with the Cuban missile crisis.

The Cuban missile crisis (13 September-20 November 1962) accentuated the East-West opposition, to the point of threatening world peace. Contrary to American imperialism, Cuba favored Communism from the early sixties and took the side of the USSR. This hostile policy towards the United States peaked in 1962, when Cuba asked its Soviet ally to protect it by installing missiles on the island. The agreement of Moscow raised tension on the US side. Indeed, the installation of these missiles constituted a threat to the United States, which was nearby. As Soviet ships carrying missiles were on their way, the Americans, who identified the installation sites in Cuba, organized a blockade of the island and warned the USSR by holding it responsible for any nuclear launch from Cuba. However, the crisis was resolved in November 1962 when, wishing to avoid nuclear war, the Soviet Union recalled its ships. On 30 June 1963, the two blocs decided to favor communication by installing a hotline between Washington and Moscow.

The East-West rivalry was also reflected in a multitude of areas, ranging from the arms race to sports during the Olympic Games, to culture, science, technology and propaganda. The conquest of space and the race to the Moon were thus the subject of true competition: indeed, it constituted a way of showing the world which power was greater than the other.

THE SOVIET CONQUEST OF SPACE

The conquest of space truly took off at the end of World War II. During this troubled period, Nazi Germany had made considerable progress in aeronautics, inventing the jet engine and ballistic missiles, including the terrible V2 missiles. These advances, although related to the military, were the starting point for space exploration. Indeed, once the war ended, many German scientists travelled to the US or the Soviet Union, nourishing the race in which the two rivals indulged.

Nevertheless, it was not until 1957 that the fun really began. On 4 October, at 11:26pm, the USSR sent the first artificial satellite into space, called Sputnik 1 ("travelling companion"). The news came as a bombshell for the United States, which had been overtaken by the Russians in this frantic quest for space. Sputnik was however an extremely simple device. It was an aluminum ball, 58cm in diameter, which had four antennas and radio transmitters and weighed about 83 kilograms. This feat fascinated the world, which listened excitedly to the "beep, beep, beep" returned by the satellite on radio waves for days.

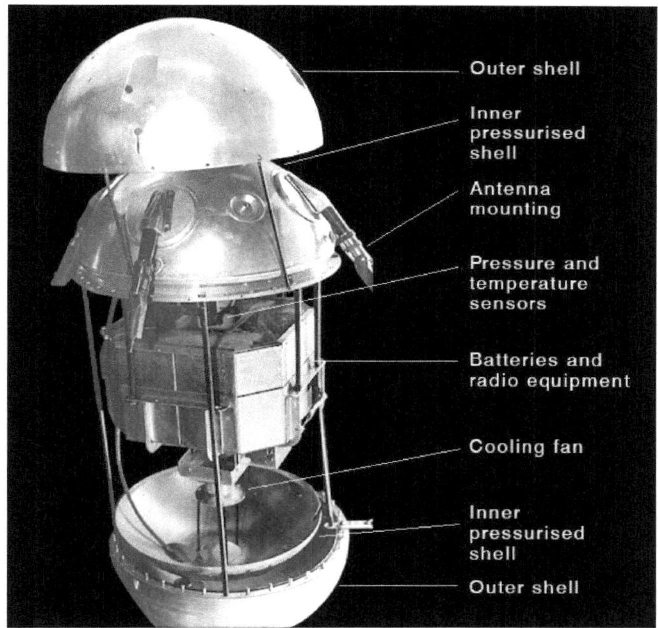

Sputnik 1.

From that day on, the Russians continued to develop their prowess, to the chagrin of the Americans. Barely a month after the launch of the first satellite, the Soviets launched Sputnik 2 with a dog, Laika, onboard, who became the first living being in space. Although she died during the mission, she proved to the world that it was possible for humans to survive being placed into orbit, as well as weightlessness. Ten more Sputniks were then sent into space, some with animals that came back alive, showing that a manned flight and a return to Earth were possible.

The Soviets also focused on the Moon in 1959 with the *Luna* probes. Although Luna 2 crashed on the natural satellite on 13 September 1959, the feat was considerable: a manmade object could reach the edge of the universe. On 4 October 1959, Luna 3 photographed the face of the satellite for the first time, which was a source of true fascination for all astronomers. Similarly, from 1961 to 1963, the Russians launched the *Venera* program designed to reach and explore another planet in the solar system: Venus.

However, a new challenge was looming on the horizon. It was now time for man to go into space. Once again, the Soviets were the first to achieve the feat by launching the *Vostok* program. On 12 April 1961, Lieutenant Yuri Gagarin (1934-1968) became the first man to go into space by performing a 108 minute journey to orbit the Earth aboard Vostok 1. Two years later, on 16 June 1963, the USSR sent the first female cosmonaut, Valentina Tereshkova (born in 1937), into space. Finally, on 18 March 1965, Lieutenant Colonel Alexei Leonov (born in 1934) completed the first spacewalk of humanity by staying out of his ship for 10 minutes.

THE US DELAY AND KENNEDY'S LEAP

For the United States, the success of Sputnik was a source of dismay. Not only was their scientific credibility at stake, but the Soviet Union now also appeared able to reach US soil through more powerful launchers. The government had no choice by to react quickly. Yet, it was not until 31 January 1958 that, after a series of failures, the first US satellite, Explorer 1, weighing just 8.5 kilos, successfully reached space, followed by Vanguard 1, dubbed the "grapefruit" by the Soviets because of its ridiculous weight of one and a half kilos.

Aware that it was falling behind, the United States created NASA on 29 July 1958, which replaced NACA (National Advisory Committee for Aeronautics). The agency was responsible for coordinating all activities and projects related to space. The Americans' delay remained significant. Imitating the USSR, they in turn sent animals into space (chimpanzees), but of course missed out on sending the first man into space. Indeed, the first flight around the Earth performed by the United States did not take place until 20th February 1962, with Lieutenant Colonel John Glenn (1921-2016) onboard.

NACA

Founded on 3 March 1915, this committee was responsible for research in aviation and aeronautics. However, with the importance of the space race, the agency was no longer enough. Therefore, it was replaced by NASA in 1958, which was also in charge of the space program.

Faced with these constant humiliations, US President John F. Kennedy (1917-1963) made a bold political gesture. In a speech before the Congress on 25 May 1961 he stated: "We choose to go to the Moon" (Chaikin 1999, p. 17). He thus presented a challenge to the world by saying that a man would set foot on the Moon by the end of the sixties, and that man would be American. The means at NASA's disposal were then enormously increased, with a staggering 25 billion dollars being invested into this space adventure that would take man to the Moon. With the *Gemini* and *Apollo* programs, the United States was gradually catching up.

THE APOLLO 11 MISSION

10 SECONDS TO GO

NASA spent almost ten years preparing to send men to the Moon. In July 1969, it was time to realize the project. The mission was to take men to the Moon onboard Apollo 11 and, according to the rotation of the NASA astronaut crew, the ship fell to the command of Neil Armstrong. He was accompanied by two teammates, Edwin "Buzz" Aldrin (born in 1930) and Michael Collins (born in 1930). For years, they underwent a battery of tests and extensive training and workouts to prepare them for the pressure of takeoffs and weightlessness. They knew their flight plan and mission by heart. All that remained was the construction of the rocket to take them there.

Crew of Apollo 11: Neil Armstrong Michael Collins and Edwin Aldrin, (from left to right).

Developed by the engineer Wernher von Braun (1912-1977), Saturn V was the largest rocket ever built. This giant pitcher had three floors, totaling 110 meters in height and, fully loaded, weighted almost 3 000 tons – 2 700 of which corresponded to the fuel (kerosene, liquid oxygen and liquid hydrogen). The structure of the rocket was somewhat like a giant thermos intended to withstand both extremely cold temperatures, caused by hydrogen and liquid oxygen, and the 2 750 °C caused by the takeoff. It also provided five gigantic F-1 engines on the first floor, whose power is still unmatched, consuming approximately 2 000 tons of fuel in the course of 2 minutes and 30 seconds. The second stage also had five J-2 engines, which although smaller could be switched off and on as needed, unlike the F-1 engines.

The third floor of the rocket also had a J-2 engine and was the most important. It was this part that contained the control and service module, as well as the lunar module. The first, called *Columbia* for Apollo 11, was the spacecraft in which the three astronauts would make their journey. Upon their return to Earth, only the control module would remain, with its large heat shield. The lunar module called *Eagle* was in turn tied to the control module during the trip. With two astronauts on board, it was detached to land on the Moon. Once the mission was complete, it took off and joined the new control module.

On 16 July 1969, everything was finally ready. Nevertheless, the mission remained extremely dangerous given the number of delicate maneuvers that needed to be performed. The three Apollo 11 astronauts knew full well that they had only one chance out of two to return to Earth alive. Yet nothing could distract them from their goal. Once strapped in the rocket, Neil Armstrong just had to wait. The countdown began. 10, 9, 8...

THE MOON OBJECTIVE

At 9:32am on 16 July 1969, five rocket engines were turned on, causing a deafening roar and making the ground shake. Over one million people made the trip to watch the takeoff. The show was breathtaking. Incandescent flame jets escaped from powerful engines. Released from the launch pad, the rocket began its meteoric rise towards space. Inside the spacecraft, the astronaut did not get to see what was happening. However, they were no less manhandled, with the acceleration of the rocket causing a force equivalent to four and a half times the Earth's gravity.

Takeoff of Apollo 11, 16 July 1969.

The first few seconds were crucial, not only for the men on the ground but for Neil Armstrong and his teammates. Indeed, nothing could stop the rocket, the speed of which continued to increase up to 4 300 km/h. A single failure could cause a fatal explosion. At 68 km off the ground, three minutes after takeoff, the first stage of the rocket was released. The five J-2 engines took over, while the first floor fell back into the Atlantic. Six minutes later the second floor detached and fell to the same fate. The thrust needed for orbit placing was colossal. On Earth, the rocket was only a tiny dot in the sky. After 11 minutes of flight, everything went as planned, and the rocket entered into orbit.

For Neil Armstrong and his companions, the view was magnificent: from their portholes they could contemplate the Earth, its continents and oceans. Before reaching the Moon, the rocket must be placed in orbit at 200 km above the ground to be in the perfect position to break away from Earth's gravity. Similarly, it was necessary to wait for a good positioning of the Moon so as to be able to reach it a few days later. Two hours and thirty minutes after takeoff, and one and a half journeys around the Earth, the translunar injection could take place. The engines were rekindled in large firing to reach the dizzying speed of 39 000 km/h. The thrust was so significant that the ship did not need to use fuel to get to the Moon. It had now fulfilled its role perfectly and could therefore hand the reins over to the *Columbia* aircraft.

The operation was critical. The *Columbia* spaceship must indeed be extracted from the third floor of Saturn V. It must then recover the lunar module still attached to the rocket. To do this, Michael Collins turned 180°. He could then proceed to gently lashing the lunar module with *Columbia*. Both modules were thus extracted from the rocket that would end up in orbit around the Sun. For Apollo 11, the mission continued. Neil Armstrong and his teammates were now en route to the moon. The journey of 385 000 km took about 72 hours, and happened without complications. The speed decreased throughout the trip. After this time, the ship had to be placed in lunar orbit. Apollo 11 reached the Moon.

"ONE SMALL STEP FOR MAN, ONE GIANT LEAP FOR MANKIND"

On 19 July 1969, after more than 75 hours of travel, Apollo 11 began its orbit around the Moon. To achieve this, the spacecraft needed to go around the natural satellite, going around its hidden side, thus cutting off communications with Earth. Neil Armstrong and his teammates were consequently alone in performing this crucial maneuver. The astronauts needed to reset the ship's engines to slow it down and force it into lunar orbit. If they did not succeed, the ship would be returned to Earth. Fortunately for the crew, everything went according to plan and entering into orbit was a success. The Moon, a hundred kilometers away from Earth, was able to be viewed up close by astronauts for the first time.

For Neil Armstrong and Buzz Aldrin, who were chosen to go down onto the surface of the Moon, the excitement continued to rise. However, they needed to wait for thirteen lunar revolutions before starting their descent. This waiting time was utilized to perform topographic features and to try to locate their landing site. After 96 hours of space travel, on 20 July, Neil Armstrong and Buzz Aldrin were inside the *Eagle* lunar module, leaving only Michael Collins in the command module. They performed one last check of all systems. They had now orbited the Moon twelve times. It was time to begin the final phase of the mission. In the control module, Michael Collins, who would continue to orbit the Moon, launched the expulsion maneuver by releasing the *Eagle*. The separation was completed without any problems and at the end of the thirteenth revolution Neil Armstrong began his descent to the Moon.

Slowly but surely, the *Eagle* approached the ground. But only a few minutes from the Moon landing, an alarm was triggered. Onboard, Neil Armstrong maintained his composure and heard from NASA that the computer of the module was overloaded. Although the mission was not interrupted, the alarm however prevented the astronaut from adjusting his position one last time to land on the Moon in the agreed area. The *Eagle* saw its fuel reserves decline, while there were only craters on the horizon, preventing any attempt to land. However, the descent continued. Finally, with only 45-50 seconds of fuel reserves left, Neil Armstrong spotted a suitable area. At 8:57pm on 20 July, the lunar module landed on the Moon, seven kilometers from the originally planned area, in what Neil Armstrong called "the Tranquility Base". On Earth, a sigh of relief was breathed. Man had just landed on the Moon.

For the astronauts, excitement was at its highest. They checked all systems and awaited discharge. When the final adjustments had been made, they put on their spacesuits and opened the module door. Neil Armstrong came out first. Meanwhile, on Earth, the event was broadcast live on global television. On 21 July, at 2:56am, Neil Armstrong set his foot on the lunar surface, becoming the first man to walk on the Moon. He then pronounced a sentence that would remain forever etched in memories: "That's one small step for man, one giant leap for mankind" (Armstrong, 1970, p. 321).

Man's first steps on the moon.

WALKING ON NEW SOIL

Once on the Moon, Neil Armstrong began the scientific observations requested by NASA. He began by describing the soil, which is powdery liked calcined coal before becoming extremely hard at about 15 centimeters deep. He then took some photographs and started collecting rock samples. Thanks to the low gravity of the Moon (1/6 of that of Earth), his movements were greatly facilitated: walking had never been so easy.

Fifteen minutes after the descent of Neil Armstrong, Buzz Aldrin descended from the module in turn. Marveling at the expanse of desert that dominated the horizon, he exclaimed: "Magnificent desolation" (Armstrong 1970 p. 327). The two astronauts then placed a small plaque, on which the two hemispheres of the Earth were represented, the signatures of the three astronauts and President Nixon (1913-1994), and the following: "Here men from the planet Earth first set foot upon the Moon, July 1969 AD. We came in peace for all mankind" (*Ibid*: 133). However, the big speeches must now give way to the scientific mission. In turn, the instruments were utilized, starting with the particle sensor of solar wind and the seismograph. The astronauts also continued to collect rock samples, to film and to take as many photographs as possible.

Meanwhile, Neil Armstrong planted the American flag in the lunar soil. In the absence of wind due to the lack of atmosphere, the flag was fitted with rigid rods, which allowed it to remain extended. Through this gesture, the Americans ratified their victory over the Soviets in the race to the Moon. Within minutes, NASA interrupted the work for an important phone call. Nixon from the White House congratulated and thanked the astronauts for their incredible success. The universe was now part of the world of men.

After exploring for 2 hours and 31 minutes, Neil Armstrong and Buzz Aldrin had exhausted their supply of oxygen. It was time to return to the lunar module.

HOUSTON, WE'RE COMING HOME

The astronauts had perfectly fulfilled their mission. It was now time to return to Earth. To do this, the lunar module must leave the ground with the help of its powerful engine. It then needed to find *Columbia* and dock in order to allow Neil Armstrong and Buzz Aldrin to return to the ship. Again, the operation was extremely delicate and two events further complicated things:

- The Columbia spaceship did not know where the lunar module was located, since it had not landed in the agreed location;
- The astronauts noticed that they had broken the power switch of the engine of the lunar module.

Fortunately, everything fell into place. NASA eventually approximately located the lunar module. As for the switch, Buzz Aldrin managed to fix it with the tip of a pen. Takeoff was planned for the 124th hour of the mission, 21 hours and 36 minutes after landing. At the agreed time, Neil Armstrong started the module engine. The *Eagle* took off.

The *Columbia* spaceship met the module and docking was completed smoothly. The three astronauts were reunited. All that remained was to return home. On 24 July 1969, Neil Armstrong and his teammates were facing the Earth. They cast off the service module 15 minutes before entering the atmosphere. What remained of *Columbia* turned into a fireball. Fortunately, the heat shield held up and their parachutes opened. At 4:51pm, after 195 hours and 19 minutes of the mission, Apollo 11 ended in the Pacific. The astronauts were then recovered by the aircraft carrier *USS Hornet*. For safety reasons, they were quarantined for 21 days in order to avoid contagion, since it remained unclear whether the Moon was barren.

The mission was therefore a success: Neil Armstrong and his companions changed the world forever.

IMPACT

TECHNOLOGICAL BENEFITS

The speech of John F. Kennedy in 1961 launched America into an incredible industrial and technical challenge, of which the economic and technological impacts were colossal. 25 billion dollars were invested in the race to the Moon, causing the collaboration of 20 000 companies and 350 000 technicians. The conquest of space was consequently an important driver of the US economy.

In addition, the Apollo 11 mission and all previous space programs undeniably contributed to the technological revolution of the second half of the 20th century. During the decade that hosted the race to the Moon, aeronautical engineers developed completely new materials, such as titanium, Kevlar, synthetic materials and the fireproof coating that helped to build rockets and spaceships. They also developed new techniques for food lyophilization, subsequently used in the food industry. Meanwhile, new technologies were emerging such as fuel cells, photovoltaic cells, solar panels, and the beginnings of GPS and the cellular phone. The same went for the area of computers, the first programming languages and the first models of which were used to tackle the complex calculations required for the Apollo missions. Even the common diapers are the products of space conquests, since astronauts had no other way to relieve themselves in space. All these advances and many others then became widespread in our society and in consumer stores.

Similarly, the field of telecommunications was forever transformed by the space race. The launch of Sputnik, in October 1957, was in fact the prelude to the launch of hundreds of satellites, the opportunities of which were enormous. In 1962, the American satellite Telstar 1 inaugurated the era of telecommunications relayed from space. Today, we are all connected to one another by GSM, GPS or the Internet, thanks to satellites that surround us. The reasoning is the same in science. Meteorology, climatology and all other environmental research are now all dependent on space technology. In recent years, the world has changed to the point of becoming dependent on spatial developments.

SPACE EXPLORATION

Besides the great technical advances, the space race and the race to the Moon also opened up an era of exploration of the universe, in order to better understand space and also our own planet. Thus, the spacecraft brought back much information about our atmosphere and the Earth's magnetic field. They even detected the presence of solar wind and its impact on the Earth's magnetosphere.

The Moon has evidently been the subject of extensive research, which has increased knowledge about the natural satellite. Dozens of both American and Soviet probes have thus brought back thousands of photographs of the two faces of the Moon. The Apollo missions, which continued until 1972, sent men to the Moon six times in order to collect new data. Throughout their missions, the astronauts on site used several scientific instruments such as magnetometers, particle detectors and seismometers to acquire a better understanding of the lunar environment.

No less than 400 kilograms of soil samples were returned to Earth. Through these studies, scientists were able to determine the chemical composition of the Moon as well as its origins, the most widespread assumption of which is a cataclysmic collision between Earth and another protoplanet (planet in the process of forming), about 4.526 billion years ago.

Finally, the study of the Moon fast became a springboard for exploring other planets and even the whole universe. In the sixties and in the coming decades, dozens of probes were sent to the four corners of our solar system to explore planets, starting with those closest – Venus and Mars – and then to observe the most distant, such as Jupiter, Saturn and Uranus. Space telescopes were in turn deflected towards the distant universe, observing the billions of stars and galaxies from Earth with unprecedented accuracy.

By setting foot on the Moon, Neil Armstrong and his successors therefore opened the doors to space exploration, pushing the boundaries of our knowledge of the world, which has continued to expand ever since.

SUMMARY

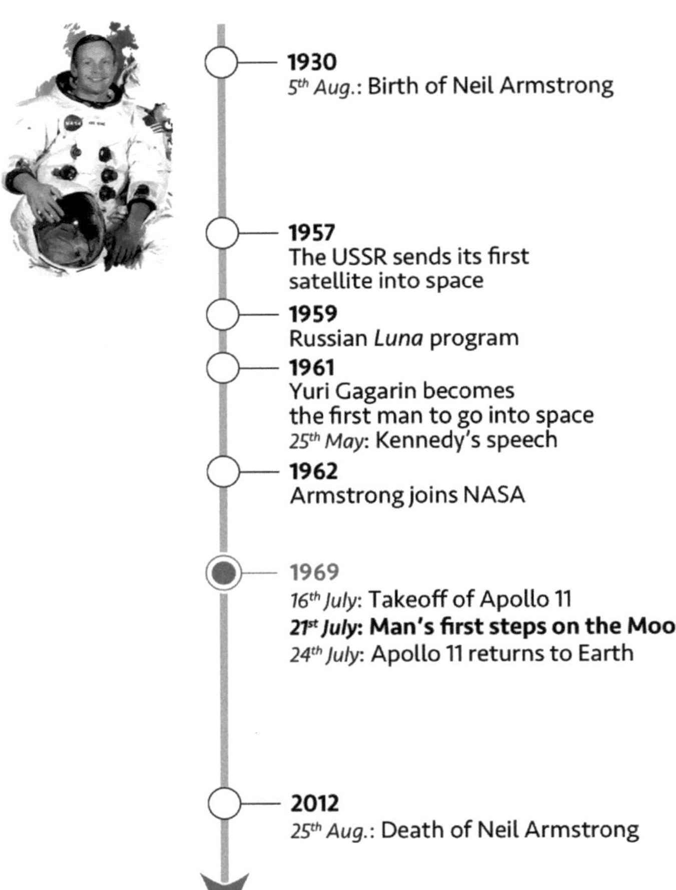

1930
5th Aug.: Birth of Neil Armstrong

1957
The USSR sends its first
satellite into space

1959
Russian *Luna* program

1961
Yuri Gagarin becomes
the first man to go into space
25th May: Kennedy's speech

1962
Armstrong joins NASA

1969
16th July: Takeoff of Apollo 11
***21st July*: Man's first steps on the Moon**
24th July: Apollo 11 returns to Earth

2012
25th Aug.: Death of Neil Armstrong

- Neil Armstrong was born on 5 August 1930 in Ohio. Passionate about aviation, he studied aeronautical engineering at Purdue University. He was enlisted in the Korean War, then returned to the United States to become a test pilot.
- In 1962, Neil Armstrong decided to join the NASA space program. Accepted by the latter, he participated in the *Gemini 8* mission in 1965. He was then selected to command the Apollo 11 mission to send men to the Moon.
- On 16 July 1969, Neil Armstrong, along with Buzz Aldrin and Michael Collins, boarded the Saturn V rocket. Liftoff was stressful for the astronauts, and within a few minutes they found themselves orbiting around the Earth.
- After completing one and a half revolutions around our planet and reaching an ideal location, the engines were switched on again to achieve a translunar injection. Neil Armstrong and his team members were then projected to the Moon. They got rid of what remained of the rocket by extracting the control module and recovering the lunar module.
- After traveling 385 000 km, which took about 72 hours, the astronauts reached the Moon. They were then placed in orbit around it in order to avoid being sent back to Earth.
- On 20 July, Neil Armstrong and Buzz Aldrin entered the lunar ship. The latter was separated from the command module and began its descent to the lunar surface. The initial landing was disturbed by the triggering of an alarm. Distracted, Neil Armstrong missed the agreed landing area and had to find a new site.
- With only 45-50 seconds of fuel remaining, the module

eventually landed on the Moon. After checking the systems, Neil Armstrong exited the vessel. On 21 July 1969 at 2:56am, he set foot on the surface, becoming the first man to walk on the Moon.

- Followed by Buzz Aldrin, Neil Armstrong began the scientific part of the mission. He took photographs, harvested sampled and installed scientific instruments. The astronauts also took the opportunity to install a commemorative plaque, plant the American flag in the ground and talk with President Nixon, who congratulated them on their achievement.
- After 2 hours and 31 minutes of exploration, the astronauts returned to the module. Hours later, they took off from the Moon and re-joined with the main spacecraft. It was now time to return to Earth.
- After this feat, Armstrong decided not to return to space. He became a professor at the University of Cincinnati and participated in the committees of inquiry for NASA.
- He died on 25 August 2012 in Cincinnati.

We want to hear from you!
Leave a comment on your online library
and share your favourite books on social media!

FIND OUT MORE

BIBLIOGRAPHY

- Armstrong, N. (1970) *Premiers sur la Lune*. Paris: Laffont.
- Chaikin, A. (1994) *A Man on the Moon: The Voyages of the Apollo Astronauts*. New York: Viking.
- Chaikin, A. (1999) *A Man on the Moon: A Giant Leap*. Alexandria: Time-Life.
- Harland, D.M. (2007) *The First Men on the Moon: The Story of Apollo 11*. New York: Praxis.
- Histoire universelle. Les guerres mondiales. (2007) *La guerre froide et la coexistence pacifique*. Paris: Hachette.
- Histoire universelle. Les guerres mondiales. (2007) *La politique des blocs*. Paris: Hachette.
- Reynaud, M.-H., Facon, P. and de la Cotardière, P. (1983) *La conquête de l'espace*. Paris: Larousse.
- Roosens, C. (2001) *Les relations internationales de 1815 à nos jours : après 1939*, Volume II. Louvain-la-Neuve: Academia-Bruylant.

ADDITIONAL SOURCES

- Hansen, J. (2012) *First Man: The Life of Neil Armstrong*. New York: Simon and Schuster.
- Mailer, N. (2015) *Moonfire: The Epic Journey of Apollo 11*. Brussels: Taschen.
- Shepard, A. (1994) *Moon Shot: The Inside Story of America's Race to the Moon*. Atlanta: Turner.
- Sparrow, G. (2007) *Spaceflight: The Complete Story from Sputnik to Shuttle and Beyond*. London: Dorling

Kindersley Limited.
* Woods, D.W. (2008) *How Apollo Flew to the Moon*. New York: Praxis.

ICONOGRAPHIC SOURCES

* Photo of Neil Armstrong taken after a flight exercise in 1960. © Nasa.
* Neil Armstrong wearing exercise clothes for Gemini 2. Royalty-free reproduction picture.
* Sputnik 1. Royalty-free reproduction picture.
* Crew of Apollo 11: Neil Armstrong, Michael Collins and Edwin Aldrin (from left to right). Royalty-free reproduction picture.
* Takeoff of Apollo 11, 16 July 1969. © Nasa.
* Man's first steps on the moon . © Nasa.

FILMS AND DOCUMENTARIES

* *Space Race*. (2005) [Documentary]. Chris Spencer and Mark Everest. Dir. UK: British Broadcasting Corporation, Mediapro Studios.
* *In the Shadow of the Moon*. (2007) [Documentary]. David Sington. Dir. USA: Discovery Films, FilmFour, Passion Pictures.
* *Moonshot*. (2008) [Documentary]. Richard Dale. Dir. USA: Dangerous Films.
* *Apollo 11: L'Aventure en direct*. (2009) [Documentary]. France: La Sept Vidéo.

COMMEMORATIVE MUSEUMS AND MONUMENTS

- Kennedy Space Center, Florida (USA).
- Commemorative star on the Hollywood Walk of Fame, Hollywood, California (USA).
- Johnson Space Center (NASA), Houston, Texas (USA).
- Armstrong Air & Space Museum, Wapakoneta, Ohio (USA).
- US Space & Rocket Center, Huntsville, Alabama (USA).

IMPROVE YOUR GENERAL KNOWLEDGE

IN A BLINK OF AN EYE !

www.50minutes.com